The Science of Marriage: What We Know That Just Isn't So

Bella DePaulo, Ph.D.

ISBN: 1508597774
ISBN-13: 978-1508597773

Do you think that getting married makes people happier and healthier and better off in all sorts of other psychological and interpersonal ways? Do you think that these are not just beliefs, but facts based on scientific research? No wonder. Celebrated scholars and authors such as Dan Gilbert and Dan Buettner have been telling us that. Judicial decisions point to those claims. Popular media narratives depend on them. There's just one problem: What we all think we know just isn't so. In THE SCIENCE OF MARRIAGE, Professor Bella DePaulo explains why these pervasive claims are just plain wrong. Dr. DePaulo is a Harvard Ph.D. with more than 100 scholarly publications. She taught graduate courses in research methods for decades. She is also the most eminent scholar of single life. If you are willing to examine beliefs that perhaps you have never questioned before, and think hard as you consider challenging arguments, read this book.

Also by BELLA DePAULO

Singled Out: *How Singles Are Stereotyped, Stigmatized, and Ignored, and Still Live Happily Ever After*

Marriage vs. Single Life: *How Science and the Media Got It So Wrong*

The Best of Single Life

Singlism: *What It Is, Why It Matters, and How to Stop It*

Single with Attitude:
Not Your Typical Take on Health and Happiness, Love and Money, Marriage and Friendship

Behind the Door of Deceit:
Understanding the Biggest Liars in Our Lives

The Hows and Whys of Lies

When the Truth Hurts: *Lying to Be Kind*

The Lies We Tell and the Clues We Miss: *Professional Papers*

Is Anyone Really Good at Detecting Lies? *Professional Papers*

Friendsight: *What Friends Know that Others Don't*

New Directions in Helping: *Volumes 1, 2, and 3*

The Psychology of Dexter

How We Live Now:
Redesigning Home and Family in the 21st Century
(forthcoming, August 2015)

CONTENTS

BELLA DePAULO

1

INTRODUCTION:

A PERSONAL NOTE ABOUT WHY I THINK THIS BOOK IS IMPORTANT

In a society as divided and contentious as our own, few beliefs are widely shared across the political and ideological spectrum. But the presumed superiority of people who get married is one of them. The idea that getting married makes people happier, healthier, better integrated into society, and more likely to live longer is taken as a given. Some of the most eminent social scientists have claimed that it is true. The premise has been incorporated into some of the most influential court rulings of our time. Programs and organizations and books and campaigns have been built around the assumption that getting married truly is psychologically and interpersonally transformative. The presumptions have contributed to the stigmatizing and shaming of millions of single people.

Before I began studying single life, I had no reason to believe the claims were not true. I love my single life, so I knew I would not be better off marrying, but I'm just one person and I thought the overall results were undoubtedly what I had always heard they were, from media reports and even fellow scientists.

Then I began reading the original research reports. I could not believe what I was finding. Most of those studies supposedly showing that getting married makes people happier or healthier or better off in any other psychological or interpersonal way – well, they were egregiously flawed, methodologically. No self-respecting social scientist should be willing to point to those studies – and there are hundreds of them – and claim that the research shows that getting married causes people to be happier or healthier. But here's the problem: Many do.

There are some daunting issues in the study of the causal implications of getting married for health and well-being. The first is that it is not possible to do the type of study that establishes causality most definitively – experimental research, in which participants are assigned at random to different conditions, such as getting married or staying single or getting divorced. So social scientists can pursue the best ethically feasible research, and report the results accurately and with appropriate acknowledgments of the limitations to the conclusions that can be drawn. But they rarely acknowledge the fundamental weaknesses of their work.

Another issue is also profoundly important and rarely, if ever, acknowledged: Even when research is conducted in the best possible ways, the results do not support the bold claims that are made about the supposedly beneficial effects of getting married. Some studies find no benefits of getting married. Others find benefits that are so qualified that no blanket statements can be made. For example, the implications of getting married often depend on whether we are talking about men or women, Blacks or Whites or other ethnic or racial groups, people who are older or younger, people who have recently married or have been married for a long time, people who have lots of economic and educational resources, and a whole host of other considerations. In still other studies, it is the people who have been single all their lives who do the best.

For more than a decade, I have been writing about the fundamental flaws of the research on the implications of getting married and describing what the results of those studies really do show. I started with my 2006 book, Singled Out: How Singles Are Stereotyped, Stigmatized, and Ignored and Still Live Happily Ever After, as well as a 2005 target article (co-authored with Wendy Morris), "Singles in society and in science," in the scholarly journal Psychological Inquiry. As the claims about the benefits of marrying continued to proliferate in social science journals and in the media, I read the original reports of every study and critiqued them in my blogs at Psychology Today and Psych Central. Still, the exaggerated, inappropriate, and false claims continued unabated.

I claim as my expertise my Ph.D. from Harvard, my scholarly publications that number more than 100, and my decades of teaching graduate courses in research methodology. But the flaws in the research used to support the claims about the benefits of marrying are so fundamental that any smart, thoughtful person should be able to recognize them. No Ph.D., no publication history, and no teaching experience are necessary.

In the fall of 2014, I wrote the paper, "No Study Has Ever Shown that Getting Married Causes People to Become Happier or Healthier – and No Study Ever Will." In it, I tried again to make the case that our beliefs about the benefits of marrying are ideological, and not based on sound science. I submitted it to a scholarly journal. It was not well-received. I was told that my tone was too problematic and I risked hurting the feelings of researchers who had made the claims about the benefits of getting married. No one expressed any concerns about the millions of single people who were falsely informed that their lives were second rate. No one raised the issue of whether people who felt unsure about marrying might be inappropriately influenced in the direction of marrying, or wondered whether those people might be especially likely to divorce later on.

I was asked to leave out huge chunks of my arguments, and soften and qualify what was left. Then, after I had essentially neutered my paper, perhaps the journal would publish it.

I declined. In my previous writings, I tried the approach of staying in my place. I used the language of academic journals, which has no attitude and no passion. I tried to be careful not to step on too many toes. It didn't work. So now it is different. I'm publishing what I want to say, in the way I want to say it.

As you get deep into the reading, you may find some of it challenging. I originally wrote it for fellow academics. But I hope you will persist anyway. If social scientists – including some of the most celebrated ones – and judges and opinion-leaders and pundits and scolds are going to continue to insist that getting married makes people happier and healthier, then they should have strong, consistent, and methodologically sound findings on their side. They don't.

--Bella DePaulo, Ph.D.
February 2015

Editor's Note:

The heart of this book, Chapter 2 ("No study has ever shown that getting married makes people happier or healthier – and no study ever will") also appears in the book, *Marriage vs. Single Life: How Science and the Media Got It So Wrong*. That collection also includes other critiques of individual studies purporting to show that getting married is transformative, and another chapter by Professor DePaulo, "Living Single: Lightening Up Those Dark, Dopey Myths."

2

NO STUDY HAS EVER SHOWN THAT GETTING MARRIED MAKES PEOPLE HAPPIER OR HEALTHIER –

AND NO STUDY EVER WILL

Summary

In the media and in academic writings, claims about the benefits of getting married are pervasive. People cannot be randomly assigned to get married or stay single or get divorced. Therefore, no study can ever support the causal claims that getting married makes people happier or healthier or better off in any other psychological or interpersonal way.

Most studies do not compare all people who have ever gotten married to those who stay single – the most appropriate comparison to make to answer the question of whether getting married results in better outcomes. Instead, only the currently married are compared to those not married. That approach greatly, and indefensibly, advantages the married group. Nonetheless, even with that built-in bias, results do not uniformly favor married people. Sometimes the always-single do best. When the married group appears to do best, often that edge is qualified by factors such as whether the adults are men or women, Black or White, younger or older, and whether the married people married recently or not so recently.

The typical social selection and social causation explanations for the purported advantages of the married group leave out significant alternatives, such as singlism. Theoretical analyses focus almost exclusively on the experiences of married people. Little has been said about the strengths of single people and the attractions of single life, leaving scholars mostly unprepared to explain the results of studies in which single people do as well as, or better than, married people.

Imagine that a pharmaceutical company has developed a new drug called Credulous and has conducted extensive testing. In all of their studies, participants get to choose whether to take the drug or not. Of those who do agree to take Credulous, close to half of them find their experiences so aversive that they refuse to continue taking the drug, even though they promised to continue for the entire length of the study.

In the research report that the drug company submits to the *New England Journal of Medicine* (NEJM), the authors set aside the people who refused to continue taking Credulous, and compare the people currently on the drug with those people not currently on the drug. They find that the people currently on the drug are doing better, and conclude that the drug is effective. In some of their analyses, the authors do not exclude the people who refused to continue taking the drug. Instead, they include those people with the people who never took the drug at all. So the analyses compare people who are currently taking the drug with everyone not currently taking the drug, including all those people who hated the drug (nearly half of those who ever tried it). They think this is entirely reasonable. If you want to know how well the drug is performing, they argue, don't you want to compare people who are currently on the drug to those who are not currently on it? So again, they find that the people currently taking Credulous are doing better than people not currently taking it, and they conclude that the drug made people better.

Would you recommend that the paper, and its conclusion about the effectiveness of Credulous, be accepted to the prestigious NEJM? Would you recommend that it be accepted to *any* journal? What if there had been a good reason to let people decide for themselves whether to take the drug or not; then would you accept the article? What if it had been submitted to you by an undergraduate taking an introductory research methods course – would you assign it a passing grade? Is there any circumstance under which you would allow researchers to set aside close to half of the people in the key condition, and compare them to everyone in the other condition(s)? This is such a violation of the most fundamental tenets of good scientific research that it seems silly even to pose the question in a serious academic journal.

The hapless pharmaceutical scientists get their paper rejected. They now understand that their cross-sectional research could never support their causal conclusions, so this time, they do something far more ambitious: They do longitudinal research. For reasons that are beyond the researchers' control, the people in their study still get to decide for themselves whether to take Credulous. The scientists start with people not on the drug, and follow them for years, assessing their health and well-being year after year. That way, they can see if outcomes change for the same people as they go from not taking the drug to taking it, and then continuing to take it. Using the same reasoning as before, they only include in their analyses the people who start taking Credulous and continue taking it over the entire course of the study. Again, they find that nearly half of the people who start taking the drug hate it and refuse to continue, and again, the scientists decide not to include them in their analyses. Now, if they find that people who take the drug feel better than they did before they started taking the drug, is it okay if they say that the drug is effective? Can they run advertisements saying that Credulous makes people feel better?

The longitudinal design is an improvement, but setting aside a substantial percentage of the people in the key group – even if it had not been nearly half – is still as indefensible, scientifically, as it was in the cross-sectional research. NEJM is unlikely to accept such a study. Teachers of undergraduates in their first research methods course might applaud their students' recognition of the superiority of a longitudinal design to a cross-sectional one, but they would still want them to understand why it is simply not acceptable, methodologically, to exclude all those people in the key group who *did* take the drug, just because they didn't like it and refused to continue to take it. You want them to realize how misleading it would be for the pharmaceutical company to advertise their drug as effective, based on studies in which the experiences of people who hated the drug are excluded. Maybe some instructors would even argue that the practice is unethical.

There should be no need to make any of these obvious points in a respectable scientific journal. When it comes to research on the implications of getting married for health and well-being, though, the need is pressing. The vast majority of studies on the topic are flawed in the fundamental ways I have described. Yet the results are used as the basis for claims that are as indefensible as the hypothetical ones made on behalf of the drug Credulous.

Researchers interested in the implications of getting married for health or well-being (or anything else) face an insurmountable methodological obstacle: It is impossible to randomly assign people to stay single or get married or get divorced or widowed. The gold standard of experimental research is out of reach. That's the main reason why no study has ever shown that getting married causes people to become happier or healthier – and no study ever will.

It is possible, though, to meet the most rigorous standards attainable within those constraints, and to be clear and accurate about the conclusions that are warranted on the basis of that research. As I will document later, bold claims about the benefits of marrying have appeared, unchallenged and often unqualified, in important legal documents, in popular publications with millions of readers, and in the lectures and writings of eminent social scientists. I will maintain that such claims are unwarranted.

My argument is not simply that it is impossible to do experimental research in which people are randomly assigned to marital statuses. I will also make the case that (1) too much of the research on marital status is not of the highest quality, even within the unavoidable restraints; (2) the prevailing designs indefensibly bias the results in favor of married people and against singles (as when people who get married and then get unmarried are excluded from the analyses); (3) even in studies in which marriage has been inappropriately advantaged, the results are not nearly as supportive of the purported benefits of marriage as many have claimed; and (4) interpretations of the results rarely acknowledge all of the serious limitations and alternative explanations. In fact, the explanations for the (presumed) marital advantage that so often appear in scholarly journals – selection and causation – routinely exclude some significant alternatives.

I will not offer an exhaustive review of outcome research on marital status; with probably thousands of relevant studies, that would be impossible. Instead, I will begin with what is perhaps the best available study of the implications of marrying (Musick & Bumpass, 2012): it is based on a nationally representative sample, it follows the same people over time, it assesses a variety of outcome variables (health, happiness, depression, self-esteem, and social ties), and analyses are reported in which everyone who married (and not just those who got married and stayed married) is included in the marriage group. Then I will consider a few illustrative studies of health and well-being. I looked for studies that are often cited in support of the supposed benefit of marrying and for studies that have certain strengths (e.g., they are longitudinal studies, or they are based on representative national samples). Studies of mortality are a special case because unlike, say, health or happiness, the ultimate outcome of death only happens once. It cannot be assessed each year as people get married or unmarried or stay single. That means that the kinds of studies that can be conducted, and the kinds of conclusions that can be drawn from those studies, are especially constrained. With those limits in mind, I will look closely at a few illustrative studies to see if marriage is really as life-extending as has been claimed.

First, though, I will document the rise of single people. Then I will offer a brief sampling of claims that getting married makes people happier or healthier or better off in other ways, before proceeding to the heart of my critique. I end with a discussion of the claims that are and are not justified, and of the vast expanse of theoretical neglect when it comes to the study of the lives of people who stay single.

The Rise of Single People

There are beliefs about single and married people that are so widely accepted, and so rarely challenged, that DePaulo and Morris (2005) have described them as ideological. There are three marriage-relevant premises of their Ideology of Marriage and Family, defined by the assumptions that (1) "just about everyone wants to marry, and just about everyone does" (p. 57); (2) "a sexual partnership is the one truly important peer relationship" and (3) "those who have a sexual partnership are better people – more valuable, worthy, and important. Compared to people who do not have the peer relationship that counts, they are probably happier, less lonely, and more mature, and their lives are probably more meaningful and more complete" (p. 58)." In a series of studies of what they called "committed relationship ideology," Day and his colleagues (Day, Kay, Holmes, & Napier, 2011) documented the system justification motives contributing to the ideology.

In the U.S., the number of people who do marry at some point in their lives has been very high – probably about 90 percent (e.g., Goldstein & Kenney, 2001). Some try it over and over again. That pattern, though, seems to be changing. The number of Americans who are not married has been increasing for decades. By 2013, 105 million adults 18 and older (44 percent) were divorced or widowed or had always been single. The majority, 62 percent, were in the latter category. When people who are cohabiting are subtracted from the 105 million, that figure decreases only to 91 million (Census Bureau News, 2014). Americans now spend more years of their adult lives not married than married (DePaulo, 2006). A recent Pew Report (Wang & Parker, 2014) used Census data to project that "when today's young adults reach their mid-40s to mid-50s, a record high share (25%) is likely to have never been married" (p. 12).

A critical question is whether people are *choosing* to live single instead of, say, getting stuck with a status they never wanted because of economic challenges, unfavorable marriage markets, or other externalities. In a study in which a representative sample of single Americans were asked whether they were in a committed relationship and whether they were looking for a partner, the biggest group, 55%, said that they were neither in such a relationship nor looking to be in one (Rainie & Madden, 2006). In another national sample (Taylor, 2010), Americans who were not married were asked whether they wanted to get married. Possible responses were yes, no, and don't know. Among those who had always been single, 58% said yes. Among the previously married, just 22% said yes.

I believe there are single people who do more than choose single life – they embrace it. I call them "single at heart" (DePaulo, 2014). By living single, people who are single at heart are living their best, most authentic, and most meaningful lives. Although my research on the topic is just preliminary, a pilot study (DePaulo, 2012) suggests that people who are single at heart differ from those who are not in extent to which they value solitude, self-sufficiency, and meaningful work. In making major changes, they prefer to make the decision that feels right to them rather than deciding with a partner. When attending social events, they prefer having a range of options (such as going on their own or with friends or not attending at all) to attending nearly always with a partner. Other differences pertain to romantic relationships. For example, people who are single at heart are especially likely to say that they are not all that interested in such relationships, and that when they have been in them, they were especially likely to feel relieved when they ended.

The Ubiquity of Claims that Marriage Improves People's Lives

Daniel Gilbert, who has won numerous prestigious awards for his research on happiness, gave a talk on the topic in 2013 to a packed room at Harvard's Peabody Museum. He asked the audience members to raise their hands if they thought that marriage leads to happiness. Addressing a man whose hand was up, Gilbert declared, "You're right." Continuing to use causal language, he said that on average, marriage "makes you happier for eight to 15 years" (Leddy, 2013).

Dan Buettner, another *New York Times* bestselling author who writes about happiness, described what he believes to be some of the most important "steps to improve our happiness." One of them was "find your soul mate" (Buettner, 2013, p. 36). His claim appeared in *AARP Magazine*, a publication with a circulation of well over 20 million.

In 2000, sociologist Linda Waite, together with Maggie Gallagher (conservative commentator and past president of the National Organization for Marriage, a group that opposed same-sex marriage), published the *The Case for Marriage: Why Married People Are Happier, Healthier, and Better Off Financially* (Waite & Gallagher, 2000). The book includes stark causal claims, such as "Marriage makes people happier" (p. 77). In *Singled Out* (DePaulo, 2006) and elsewhere (e.g., DePaulo & Morris, 2005), I critiqued those assertions, including more specific claims about the results of particular studies. Nonetheless, the book has been cited in dozens of scholarly journal articles – nearly always uncritically.

Claims about the purported benefits of getting married have made it into high-profile legal decisions. For example, after Californians voted in 2008 for Proposition 8, which banned same-sex marriage, a Federal District Court in San Francisco struck down the ban two years later (Perry v. Schwarzenegger, 2010). The ruling included this claim: "Marriage benefits both spouses by promoting physical and psychological health" (p. 69), followed by seven paragraphs of similarly worded claims.

In the academic literature on marital status, claims about the benefits of marrying are pervasive. Typically, a few studies are cited – or perhaps Waite and Gallagher (2000) is referenced to legitimate the claims – and then the authors move on to speculate as to why getting married is so advantageous or to introduce their new study of the purported benefits of marrying. But what do those studies really demonstrate, when held to the basic standards of acceptable scientific research?

What is the evidence that getting married makes people happier or healthier or better off in any other psychological or interpersonal way? I will take a brief look at some cross-sectional research, then focus primarily on research on transitions from being single to getting married for the first time. I will also consider transitions from marriage to divorce. I will discuss cohabitation, separation, and widowhood in much less detail. Parental status is a separate issue from marital status; my interest here is in the latter. The literature on family structure (e.g. outcomes of children in single parent vs. two-parent families) suffers from many of the same methodological challenges as the research on marital status (see DePaulo, 2006) but that is not the focus of this article.

Multiple Outcomes Over Time: Implications of Getting Married for Happiness, Health, Depression, Self-Esteem, and Social Ties

Most studies of marital status focus on just one outcome variable, or one type of outcome. Too many are cross-sectional. Almost all of them compare only those people who are currently married (or, in longitudinal research, those who get married and stay married) to people who are not married. Perhaps the only exception to all three of these limitations is Musick and Bumpass's (2012) analyses of the first two waves of data from the National Survey of Families and Households (NSFH). Outcome variables were happiness, health, depression, self-esteem, and social ties (contact with parents, time spent with friends, and relationship quality with parents).

The authors began with the adults who were under age 50 and single (not married and not cohabiting) during the first wave of data collection, 1987-1988. By the time of the second wave about six years later, 1992-1994, some had stayed single, others transitioned to cohabitation, and others to marriage – some directly and others after first cohabiting. The authors compared changes in each of the outcome variables for each of the groups making a transition to the changes for those who stayed single. The single group did not just include those who had always been single; previously married people who were not cohabiting were also included. That is important, since research sometimes shows less favorable outcomes among the previously married than among the currently married or the always-single (e.g., DePaulo, 2006; DePaulo & Morris, 2005; Rook & Zettel, 2005).

Previous research has documented decreases over time in the quality of marital and cohabiting relationships (e.g., Brown, 2003; Umberson, Williams, Powers, Chen, & Campbell, 2005), as well as a honeymoon effect for well-being, such that people who marry experience an initial increase that soon dissipates (e.g., Lucas, Clark, Georgellis, & Diener, 2003). To test for possible differences in outcomes for earlier vs. later years of unions (marriage or cohabitation), Musick and Bumpass (2012) looked separately at recent unions (formed within the previous 3 years) and older ones (formed within the previous 4-6 years).

The authors first reported the usual analyses, in which only those people who got married (or began cohabiting) and stayed together were included. In these analyses, biased in favor of marriage because of the exclusion of all those people who got married but did not stay that way, and because of the inclusion of the previously married with the always-single, the authors found that: (1) there were no differences in health – i.e., people who got married, either directly or after cohabiting, did not become any healthier over time than did the people who stayed single; there were no differences in (2) self-esteem or in (3) quality of relationships with parents; people who got married did become (4) happier and (5) less depressed; people who married, either directly or after cohabiting, (6) had less contact with their parents and (7) spent less time with their friends. The findings for social ties are consistent with previous cross-sectional studies of nationally representative samples (Gerstel, 2011; Gerstel & Sarkisian, 2006); in that research, people who have always been single were most likely to contact, visit, advise, and support their parents and siblings, and the currently-married were least likely to do so. Singles were also the most likely to help, encourage, and socialize with their friends and neighbors.

In the analyses in which all those who got married were included in the married group, even if their union dissolved, and in which the changes over all six years were considered together (rather than broken down into the more recent vs. older unions), people who got married (without first cohabiting) became no happier, no healthier, and showed no greater increases in self-esteem than those who stayed single; the quality of their relationships with their parents was not different either. Only on the depression measure did the married group fare better. The married group did worse with regard to social ties: over time, they had less contact with their parents and spent less time with their friends than did those who stayed single. Those who transitioned from cohabiting to marrying showed no greater improvements in health or self-esteem than those who stayed single; they did become happier and less depressed. Again, they fared worse than the singles with regard to staying in touch with their parents and spending time with friends.

Separate analyses of the more recent unions and the older ones showed that the short-term implications of marrying were positive for some outcomes: Those who had married (or transitioned into cohabitation) within the previous three years were happier, healthier, less depressed, and had higher self-esteem than those who stayed single. There were no differences in the quality of relationships with parents. Those who got married again fared worse on social ties: Over time, they had less contact with their parents and spent less time with their friends.

Any positive outcomes of marrying that show up after just a few years could be just honeymoon effects. Do the positive outcomes endure, and do the negative ones dissipate? In the analyses of the more enduring unions, the authors found that when those who had married (or transitioned into cohabitation) between four and six years ago were compared to those who stayed single, there were *no differences in happiness, health, depression, self-esteem, or relationship quality with parents;* the only significant effects favored single people: they had more contact with their parents and spent more time with their friends.

In the analyses showing some results favoring married people, none of the effects were large. The authors noted that the largest of all of the effects (regardless of which group they favored) were about one-third of a standard deviation and that most effects were smaller. For example, in the analyses including all people who got married (and not broken down by more recent vs. more enduring unions), there were only three significant effects favoring those who married. The decrease in depression for those who married directly was just .12 standard deviations; the increase in happiness and decrease in depression for those who married after cohabiting were both .25 standard deviations.

Getting Married and (Not) Getting Happier, More Satisfied, or Less Depressed

Cross-sectional studies of happiness, life satisfaction, and other measures of subjective well-being are sometimes cited in support of the claim that married people are happier. For example, in a national sample of adults who rated their happiness on a 1-4 point scale, with higher numbers indicating greater happiness, mean happiness ratings were 3.3 for the currently married, 3.2 for the always-single, and 2.9 for both the divorced and the widowed (Gove & Shin, 1989). As is typical, the married group excludes all those people who got married but did not stay that way. Even with that advantage accorded to the married group, the lowest levels of happiness were reported not by those people who had stayed single but instead by those who were previously married. With regard to the question of whether getting married improves happiness (which can only be addressed in the most suggestive way by cross-sectional data), the most relevant comparison is between all people who had ever married and those who stayed single. I have never seen such a comparison reported in a cross-sectional study. It is a straightforward matter to compute the weighted means, though, and in this study, they are the same, 3.2 for both groups.

Over time, the more methodologically sophisticated longitudinal studies have become much more commonplace. Some are prospective studies, in which well-being is assessed repeatedly, beginning before the wedding and continuing for years afterwards. In a meta-analytic review, Luhmann and her colleagues (2012) analyzed 18 independent samples in which the measures of subjective well-being included cognitive well-being (e.g., ratings of life satisfaction), affective well-being (e.g., ratings of happiness or depressed mood), and relationship satisfaction. (The Musick & Bumpass study, with just two data points several years apart, was not included.) On the average, there were 5 assessments and the first was taken an average of four months before the wedding.

Studies of cognitive well-being showed that ratings of life satisfaction were significantly higher just after the wedding than they were before. Over time, though, life satisfaction continued to decline until it was no greater than it was the first time it was measured, when the participants were single. This is the familiar pattern known as the honeymoon effect. The three studies of affective well-being found no effect at all of getting married – there was no honeymoon effect and no subsequent changes in happiness or depressed mood. Studies of relationship satisfaction found that those assessments were more negative just after the wedding than they were before, and they continued to decline over time. Another 20 independent samples of post hoc research (in which the first assessment was not made until just after the wedding) also showed that relationship satisfaction decreased continuously over time.

Some of the studies in the meta-analysis were designed to test the set-point theory of adaptation to life events, and for that reason included only those people who got married for the first time and stayed married over the course of the study. A better test of the implications of getting married for happiness or depressed mood or life satisfaction is offered by those few studies in which people were included in the analyses even if they did not stay married. Results of those studies were not reported separately but they were compared to the results of the studies in which included only those people who stayed married. The decline in subjective well-being in the years after the wedding was even greater for the more inclusive studies than it was for those including only people who stayed married.

The meta-analytic results are not very supportive of claims that getting married makes people happy. Affective well-being, including happiness and depressed mood, showed no improvement at all, not even a short-lived honeymoon effect, and relationship satisfaction, on the average, went nowhere but down. Only life satisfaction increased initially, and that effect did not last. It dissipated especially quickly in studies in which everyone who got married was included, even if they did not stay married.

Was there some way that researchers could still claim that marriage mattered in a positive way? One approach that has been used is to estimate the levels of well-being that participants would have experienced if they had stayed single instead of marrying. In an analysis of British data, Yap, Anusic, and Lucas (2012) found in their normative analyses that both single and married people reported life satisfaction ratings that decreased every year. Those who got married and stayed married, they found, had higher ratings than they would have if they had stayed single. As the authors explained, "...although our previous analyses showed that people were no happier after marriage than they were before, these results suggest that married people are indeed happier than they would have been if they did not get married. This is because if they did not get married their life satisfaction would have decreased even more due to normative declines in life satisfaction common to both married and single groups" (p. 484). (See also Anusic, Yap, & Lucas, 2014a and 2014b, for similar analyses of datasets from Australia and Switzerland.)

The meta-analytic results are not very supportive of claims that getting married makes people happy. Affective well-being, including happiness and depressed mood, showed no improvement at all, not even a short-lived honeymoon effect, and relationship satisfaction, on the average, went nowhere but down. Only life satisfaction increased initially, and that effect did not last. It dissipated especially quickly in studies in which everyone who got married was included, even if they did not stay married.

One problem with this conclusion about people who got married is that it is based on a sample of only those people who got married and stayed married. So we can't say, on the basis of that analysis alone, that "married people are indeed happier than they would have been if they did not get married." But what if we limit the claim to people who got married and stayed married? Then can we say that getting married made them happier?

The people who got married and stayed married are different people than the ones who stayed single, so we don't really know whether they would have been less satisfied with their lives if they stayed single. Maybe they are the kinds of people who would have resisted the usual declines in life satisfaction even if they had not married. But suppose the authors are correct in their suggestion that the people who got married and stayed married were more satisfied than they would have been if they stayed single. What does that mean for the key causal question at the heart of this article – does getting married make people happier or more satisfied? If the people who stayed single had instead married, would they have become more satisfied with their lives?

Remember that the people who got married *chose* to do so. What about the people who stayed single? From national surveys, we know that substantial numbers of people are choosing to live single (Rainie & Madden, 2006; Taylor, 2010). Maybe some are not just choosing single life but eagerly embracing it (DePaulo, 2014). Can we really assume that if those people had been nudged or forced or randomly assigned to marry that they would have become more satisfied with their lives?

Getting Married and (Not) Getting Healthier

An example of cross-sectional research on marital status and health is the National Health Interview Survey, in which a different representative sample of adults in the U.S. was questioned every year beginning in 1972. They self-reported their health as poor, fair, good, or very good/excellent. Liu and Umberson (2008) analyzed marital status differences through 2003. Their dependent variable was not mean health scores but the predicted probability that people in a particular group reported health that was good or excellent.

Remember that the people who got married chose to do so. What about the people who stayed single? From national surveys, we know that substantial numbers of people are choosing to live single (Rainie & Madden, 2006; Taylor, 2010). Maybe some are not just choosing single life but eagerly embracing it (DePaulo, 2014). Can we really assume that if those people had been nudged or forced or randomly assigned to marry that they would have become more satisfied with their lives?

The authors compared five marital status groups – currently married, always-single, separated, divorced, and widowed – overall, and then separately by gender and by race (African-Americans vs. non-Hispanic whites). They found that "the married remain more likely than any other group to report good health for both men and women over the entire study period." They also showed that over time, the difference between the always-single and the currently-married steadily decreased, while the difference between the currently-married and each of other groups (separated, divorced, and widowed) actually increased over time.

The study generated plenty of press, including, for example, the *Washington Post* headline, "Married Folks Still the Healthiest" (Gordon, 2008). Readers might think the lesson is that if they want to be healthy, they should get married. Of course, for all of the usual reasons, that inference cannot be drawn from the research. The married group consisted not of everyone who ever married, but only those who were currently married. Those who got married and then got unmarried reported worse health than those who were currently married; for at least the last 15 years of data, they also reported worse health than those who stayed single. This pattern, in which the always-single people fare most similarly to the currently-married, and the previously married fare the worst, is the same pattern often found in cross-sectional research on happiness. In their review of various measures of physical health, Rook and Zettel (2005) came to the same conclusions. (See also DePaulo, 2006, for a review of many different health measures from CDC data.)

In their review articles, their introductions to empirical articles, and in their summaries in textbooks, authors may be tempted to grab onto the statement of the superiority of the currently-married group over all the others. Let's consider the specifics of those differences for the most recent year for which the data were analyzed, 2003. The probability of reporting good or excellent health for the currently married was .929 (see the graph on p. 246). For those who had always been single, it was .926. Remember that the currently-married group is already advantaged because those who married and then got unmarried have been removed. Even so, their health advantage over all those who stayed single was the difference between .929 and .926.

Among African-Americans, not even that tiny difference appeared; in 2003, the health of the African-Americans who had always been single was identical to the currently-married. With regard to gender differences, a comparison of the separate graphs for women and men (across race) shows that in 2003, the women who had always been single reported better heath than the men who were currently married.

Liu and Umberson (2008) ended their article with an important note of caution: "encouraging marriage in order to promote health may be misguided. In fact, getting married increases one's risk for eventual marital dissolution, and marital dissolution seems to be worse for self-rated health now than at any point in the past three decades" (p. 252).

As indicated in the previous section, the research literature on the implications of marrying for subjective well-being includes many longitudinal studies with numerous waves of assessment. The same is not true of the literature on physical health. Some of the studies compared the same people at just two different points in time. Still, compared to the cross-sectional research, the available studies allow for stronger inferences about the health implications of marrying.

In one example, Williams and Umberson (2004) analyzed data from a nationally representative sample of Americans 24 and older surveyed between 1986 and 1994. They rated their health on a 5-point scale. The authors created a dependent variable that was the predicted probability of reporting excellent or very good health (the top two of the 5 points). When single people who got married (for the first time) were compared to single people who stayed single, the men – but not the women – reported significantly better health. When those who were single throughout the course of the study were compared to those who were married the whole time, there were no differences at all in health for either the men or the women. Overall, those who got divorced were more likely to report improvements in their health relative to those who stayed married. For men, age mattered: health improved for younger men who divorced, but it got worse for older men. For women, getting divorced did not compromise their health at any age.

In another example, Wu and Hart (2002) analyzed two-year intervals of longitudinal data from a representative sample of Canadians between 20 and 64. Their physical health measures were an index of overall functional health (dexterity, mobility, vision, hearing, speech, cognition, emotion, and pain and discomfort) and a self-report of health status. They found that single people who got married reported no better health on either measure than the people who stayed single; the results were true of both the men and the women. Something else was true for both the men and the women: Those who stayed married over the two-year intervals reported significantly *worse* health on both measures than those who stayed single. Men who got divorced reported worse health on both measures than men who stayed single; for women, there were no differences.

So does getting married make people healthier? None of the studies we can conduct in an ethical way would allow us to answer that question in the strongest way possible, methodologically. The evidence available from the studies that have been done provides a tangle of non-results and qualified effects. Cross-sectional comparisons that advantage married people by including only the currently married in the group sometimes show only the tiniest differences between that group and the always-single group, or, in certain comparisons (such as with African Americans), no differences at all (Liu & Umberson, 2008; Rook & Zettel, 2005). The divorced group – people who did get married at one time – typically have worse health than people who stay single, a difference that appears to be increasing over time (Liu & Umberson, 2008). Comparisons over time show that single people who get married (either directly or after cohabiting) show either no improvements in health (Musick & Bumpass, 2012), or improvements only for the men (Williams & Umberson, 2004), or improvements only for the first few years and only if those who transitioned to cohabiting relationships and stayed in those relationships are included in the analyses (Musick & Bumpass, 2012). Comparisons of those who have settled into their marital statuses are even more troublesome for the "get married, get healthy" hypothesis: those who stay married for years are either no healthier (Williams & Umberson, 2004) or less healthy (Wu & Hart, 2002) than those who stay single.

There are many other studies of marital status and health. From just this brief sampling of some of the best, though, it already seems clear that getting married is no surefire path to better health, and should not be described as such.

Getting Married and (Not) Living Longer

To study the implications of getting married for outcomes such as health or happiness, it is possible to follow the same people over time, assessing them year after year. That way, we can see what happens when, for example, people transition from being single to married, or married to divorced. We can track experiences (health, happiness, etc.) leading up to the event, around the time of the event, and in the years afterwards. It is from those kinds of studies that we have seen that any positive implications of marrying sometimes amount to little more than a short-lived honeymoon effect.

When the outcome of interest is mortality, though, the analytic possibilities are more limited. Since death is a one-time thing, we cannot track people's rate of dying as they stay single or get married or get divorced. Brockman and Klein (2004), however, have used the German panel study (ongoing since 1984) to estimate how marital biography might predict mortality. Because the study is so large and has been going on for so long, enough people have died to make mortality estimates possible.

Beginning with cross-sectional analyses, the authors compared the relative mortality risks of the currently single, divorced, and widowed people to the currently married. The married group, therefore, does not include anyone who ever married but only those who are currently married. Their measure was a hazard ratio, indicating the relative risk of mortality for the group in question as compared to the reference group. (Values greater than 1.0 indicate a greater relative risk of dying relative to the reference group, whereas values lower than 1.0 indicate a smaller risk.) The findings did not spell uniform doom for single people. Once selection effects were controlled, the mortality risk for the single men was no different than for the currently-married men. The divorced men had a marginally higher risk than the currently married men. For the women, the currently single did have a higher risk but the divorced women's mortality risk was no different from that of the currently married women.

Next the authors asked whether mortality risks might change over time – for example, as people stay married longer or as more years pass since they divorced. In a key table (Table 3, p. 577), the authors showed the hazard ratios for men and women who had been married (for the first time) for 0-2 years, 2-7 years, and more than 7 years. They also showed the hazard ratios separately for men and women who had been divorced (for the first time) for 0-2 years, 2-7 years, and more than 7 years. The reference group was same-aged people who had stayed single. Again, they controlled for selection effects. The biggest hazard ratio – i.e., the greatest risk of dying – occurred during the first two years of marriage. For men, it was 3.10 and for women, it was 2.44. Getting married seems to more than double or triple the mortality risk during the first two years, compared to staying single. After the second year, none of the effects were significant for the men or the women –

the relative mortality risk did not differ from 1.0. Getting divorced also mattered in a negative way at first – in the first two years, it more than doubled the mortality risk for men (2.33) and for women (2.32) compared to staying single. The effect of divorce also dissipated over time. For men, it was no longer significant between 2-7 years after the divorce, or beyond 7 years. For women, it was no longer significant after 7 years; between 2 and 7 years, mortality risk was significantly lower.

In an American longitudinal study, nearly 300,000 people who were at least 45 years old at the start of the study were tracked for up to 11 years (Johnson, Backlund, Sorlie, & Loveless, 2000). The familiar comparisons were used – those who were divorced, widowed, or had always been single at the start of the study were compared to those who were currently married. The abstract made the results seem straightforward: "Each of the non-married categories show elevated RR of death compared to married persons..." (RR is relative risk.) But were all of the unmarried groups really more likely to die younger than the married group?

The authors computed mortality risk for eight different groups: men and women who were Black or White, and, when first assessed, were either between 45 and 64 or 65 and older. Looking first at the people who had always been single, their mortality risk did not differ from the currently-married in three of the four groups of Blacks. (The exception was the younger Black men.) For whites, the always-single groups did have higher mortality risks than the currently-married group. Now let's look at the eight divorced groups. Seven of them have a significantly higher mortality risk than the currently married. (Older Black men were the exception.) Now let's compare the mortality risk (relative to the currently married) of the always-single and the divorced. In seven of the eight comparisons, the divorced had the same or higher mortality risks than the always-single. (Younger white single women had a slightly higher mortality risk than the young white divorced women.)

Does the American study show that if you get married, you will live longer? Not if you are a Black woman or an older Black man. Not if you get married and then get divorced (unless you are an older Black man). Suppose that every comparison of the always-single to the currently married had favored the currently-married people. Then could we say that getting married makes people live longer? Again, no, because in 7 of the 8 groups, the people who married and then divorced did not live longer. Even if everyone who ever got married (and not just the currently married) lived longer than those who stayed single, we could not know for sure that if the single people had married, they would have lived longer. They were different people than the ones who chose to marry.

There are many studies of marital status and mortality. One after another compares only a select group of people who got married to all of the people who stayed single. Those who got married and then got unmarried are excluded from the married group, thereby biasing the results in favor of marriage. Even with that advantage afforded to the married group, the always-single people do not always have higher mortality rates.

Results of a longitudinal study showed that those who had been married for at least four years were not doing any better in any way than those who had stayed single. They were no happier, healthier, or less depressed, and they had no higher self-esteem. They did, though, have less contact with their parents and friends.

Conclusions

Does getting married make people happier or healthier or better off in any other social or psychological way? Because we cannot randomly assign people to marital statuses, we can never answer that causal question in a definitive way. Causal claims about marriage "making" people happier or healthier should not be made in the media, and of course, they should not appear in scholarly publications.

Keeping in mind that the conclusions we draw from the research we can do on the implications of marrying can only be described as suggestive and not definitive, what does the available research suggest? In the media and in scientific publications, claims that getting married is beneficial are rampant. But what do the data actually suggest? One of the most common approaches to the study of the implications of marrying is a cross-sectional one, in which people who are currently married are compared to other unmarried groups such as people who are divorced or widowed or have always been single. As an answer to the question of whether getting married makes people better off, such comparisons give an unfair and scientifically indefensible advantage to the married group, which includes not all people who ever got married – the appropriate group to use to answer the question of whether getting married will make you better off – but only those who got married and stayed married. Since the divorced group often fares worse than the currently-married group – *and* worse than the group of people who have always been single, the common decision to remove them from the marriage group is particularly egregious.

And yet, even though the deck is stacked in favor of the currently-married group in such research, that group still does not fare all that well in comparison to the always-single group. Differences favoring the currently-married group are sometimes tiny. Sometimes they depend on whether the people in question are male or female, Black or white, or younger or older.

Increasingly, studies of the implications of marrying are longitudinal, and those designs allow stronger inferences than cross-sectional designs. Still, in the vast majority of the studies of lives over time, the same biased comparisons are used. The married group typically consists of only those people who got married (often for the first time) and stayed married over the course of the study, and that group is compared to other not-married groups. Such comparisons are never the most appropriate ones if the goal is to answer the question of whether getting married improves people's lives. Yet even when such an unfair advantage is accorded to the married group, the results provide at best a muddled answer to the question.

In some ways, people who stay single do better than those who marry. For example, they have more contact with their friends and their parents. Sometimes getting married results in no benefits at all compared to staying single – for example, there may be no boost to self-esteem, health, happiness, or depressed mood. When getting married does result in improvements relative to staying single, those findings are often not generalizable across groups but instead depend on whether the people in question are male or female, Black or white, younger or older, and whether the people who got married have been married for just a few years or for longer. Longitudinal studies comparing people who remain in their particular marital status over time also fail to support claims about the benefits of marriage: those who stay married do no better, or sometimes even worse, than those who stay single.

The more appropriate analyses, in which all those people who ever married are compared to those who stay single, are rare. Results of such analyses suggest that any findings favoring people who get married become weaker or disappear entirely. For example, Musick and Bumpass (2012) found that those who had been married between four and six years were not doing any better in any way than those who had stayed single. They were no happier, healthier, or less depressed, and they had no higher self-esteem. They did, though, have less contact with their parents and friends.

The studies I reviewed are a selected subset, chosen to illustrate my points using studies that have often been cited in the literature, or studies that are particularly strong (for example, because they are longitudinal, based on representative national samples, or include an array of measures). If I had reviewed more studies, I would have needed to add even more qualifications to the claim that getting married improves people's lives (DePaulo, 2011a). For example, in a study of depression, Frech and Williams (2007) compared only those who got married and stayed married to those who stayed single. They found that those who got married became less depressed than those who stayed single if the focus was on the 20 percent of the people who were already depressed before they got married, or if it was on those who, once married, experienced greater than average marital happiness.

When researchers exclude from the married group those who got married but did not stay that way, sometimes they acknowledge their decision and its implications. For example, in a longitudinal test of "the assumption that marriage enhances well-being" (p. 895), Horwitz, White, and Howell-White (1996) excluded from their sample people who got married and then separated or divorced. "We do not include this group," they explained, "because they clearly are not deriving any benefits of marriage" (p. 899).

There are other ways, too, that researchers advantage the married group in ways that would not be acceptable in research on any other topic. For example, when Hawkley and her colleagues (2008) found no differences in loneliness between currently-married people and currently unmarried people, they then compared to all of the unmarried people just those married people who considered their spouse to be a confidant. Apparently, neither the editor nor any of the reviewers noted that the married and unmarried groups were no longer comparable, as they might be if, for instance, the single group included only those unmarried people who considered their closest friend or relative to be a confidant. More generally, the claim is sometimes made that it is not marriage that is beneficial, but "healthy marriages" or happy ones (e.g., Parker-Pope, 2010). Perhaps this is the rationale for including only the happiest or healthiest couples in the married group, and comparing them to all single people, regardless of their health or happiness. As social scientists, we should question such practices. None of us, for example, would recommend publication of a study in which the manufacturer of a weight-loss drug compared people on their drug who were also exercising to people on the competing drug, regardless of whether they were exercising.

We are left with the insurmountable methodological obstacle we started with: People cannot be randomly assigned to marital status. They get to choose. We just don't know whether people who choose to stay single would have fared better if they were randomly assigned to marry; the marriage data is based on different data – data from people who chose to marry.

The tradition of comparing only those people who are currently married to various groups of currently-unmarried people (either separately or combined, either in cross-sectional or longitudinal designs) is so much a part of the literature on marital status that, sadly, I expect it to continue. Those scholars who do continue to make statements about how the currently married compare to other groups should also address another question: "And so?" Imagine, for example, that a study finds that currently married people are faring better in some way than people who have always been single (or people who are divorced or widowed or separated). What is the answer to the question, "And so?" Is it that the unmarried people should get married? No, because the currently married group does not include all of the people who ever got married. Does it mean that the unmarried group should get married and stay married? We can't say that either. Suppose all those people in intensely hostile, conflict-ridden, and sometimes even abusive marriages had stayed married instead of divorcing: Do we know that they then would have been better off? No, we don't. Then is the answer to the "So what" question that the unmarried group should continue to marry and divorce, marry and divorce, until they find a marriage that makes them happy and healthy? But then what about the potentially adverse effects of all of those transitions?

Suppose, then, that researchers begin to compare all those who ever married to those who stayed single. If they then find that the ever-married group fares better than the ever-single group, does that mean that single people should get married if they want the same benefit? It is a far better design than the one in which only those who got married and stayed married are skimmed off the top of the ever-married group. Still, we are left with the insurmountable methodological obstacle we started with: People cannot be randomly assigned to marital status. They get to choose. We just don't know whether people who *choose* to stay single would have fared better if they were randomly assigned to marry; the marriage data is based on different data – data from people who *chose* to marry.

Have researchers simply assumed, consistent with the Ideology of Marriage and Family (DePaulo & Morris, 2005) that of course just about all single people wish they were married and would fare better if they did marry? If social scientists did a study in which engineers were found to be more satisfied with their lives than poets, would they then conclude that if only the poets became engineers, they would become more satisfied with their lives?

Have researchers simply assumed, consistent with the Ideology of Marriage and Family (DePaulo & Morris, 2005) that of course just about all single people wish they were married and would fare better if they did marry? If social scientists did a study in which engineers were found to be more satisfied with their lives than poets, would they then conclude that if only the poets became engineers, they would become more satisfied with their lives?

Doesn't the approach I'm suggesting, in which everyone who ever married is compared to those who stay single, make it harder to answer the kinds of questions that have interested marriage researchers? Suppose, for example, we want to learn whether the supposedly greater availability of social support in marriage, relative to single life, is linked to better health outcomes. How can we learn about social support in marriage if we include in the marriage group people who were once married but are currently divorced? They are no longer getting any ongoing social support from their marriages. Doesn't that justify the longstanding tradition of comparing only those who are currently married to some unmarried group? If you want to make that argument, then you also need to agree with the drug companies who want to make claims for the effectiveness of their drugs based solely on people who choose to take it and to continue to take it, while setting aside 43 percent of the people who tried the drug and refused to continue with it. (I'm using 43 percent as an approximation of the divorce rate [Amato, 2010].) Would you sign your name to a review for the NEJM recommending publication of such a study?

Here is another way to think about it. In a longitudinal study of marital status and health, 10,000 Dutch adults were asked about 13 possible health complaints and 23 chronic conditions. The married participants who reported at least four complaints were at least 1.5 times more likely to be divorced after 4.5 years (the end of the study) and those who reported at least two chronic conditions were twice as likely to be divorced by then (Joung, Van de Mheen, Stronks, van Poppel, & Mackenbach, 1998). That's just one study, of course, but knowing that this is an empirically-demonstrated possibility, do you still want to compare only the people who are currently married to people who are unmarried and then try to figure out what it is about marriage that is "making" people healthier?

Suppose you are not dissuaded by anything I've argued so far. You want to continue to include in the married group only those who got married and stayed married. You think it is fine to set aside the 43 percent who disliked their marital experience so much that they refused to continue to stay married. Then how about if I use the same logic in my studies of single people? I want to know about the health implications of staying single. I decide to exclude from my single group the 43 percent who are least happy with their single lives. That's only fair – it is not as if single people can unilaterally decide to marry the way married people can unilaterally decide to file for divorce. If I submitted a paper to a prestigious journal in which I claimed the health superiority of single people based only on the top 57 percent of single people, would you accept it for publication? Would you recommend acceptance to the least prestigious journal?

The tradition of comparing only those people who are currently married to various groups of currently-unmarried people (either separately or combined, either in cross-sectional or longitudinal designs) is so much a part of the literature on marital status that, sadly, I expect it to continue. Those scholars who do continue to make statements about how the currently married compare to other groups should also address another question: "And so?" Imagine, for example, that a study finds that currently married people are faring better in some way than people who have always been single (or people who are divorced or widowed or separated). What is the answer to the question, "And so?" Is it that the unmarried people should get married? No, because the currently married group does not include all of the people who ever got married. Does it mean that the unmarried group should get married and stay married? We can't say that either. Suppose all those people in intensely hostile, conflict-ridden, and sometimes even abusive marriages had stayed married instead of divorcing: Do we know that they then would have been better off? No, we don't. Then is the answer to the "So what" question that the unmarried group should continue to marry and divorce, marry and divorce, until they find a marriage that makes them happy and healthy? But then what about the potentially adverse effects of all of those transitions?

What Do the Findings Tell Us about the Lives of Single and Married People? Theoretical and Conceptual Issues

The belief that married people are better off than single people is so widespread and so rarely challenged that scholars have gone on to address the next question: Why is it that married people do better? Most explanations are categorized as either "social selection" or "social causation." Social selection is the possibility that people who are, say, happier or healthier are more likely to get married or stay married than are people who are less happy or healthy. This is typically the explanation that researchers want to rule out, so as to find support for the preferred causal hypothesis. If married people were already happier or healthier than single people even before they married, then marriage can't be credited with any better outcomes of the currently-married group. Similarly, if less healthy or less happy people are less likely to stay married, then again, that complicates the case for the claim that it is marriage that is "making" people healthier or happier.

Differences on the outcome measure of interest are the most obvious selection variables to be considered, but any other variable that could account for the differences in outcomes between the various marital status groups are also important. That's why demographic variables such as age, income, and education are so often included as controls in marital status research. But trying to equate the currently-married group to one or more of the non-married groups by statistical controls is never going to be wholly satisfying. Researchers may not even think of all of the possible variables that could be relevant, and even if that were possible, the number of variables that can be simultaneously included in an analysis is limited. Statistical controls fall short of random assignment as a way of ruling out alternatives, and again, random assignment to marital statuses is something we just cannot do. We are inevitably left with different kinds of people – those who chose to marry and those who are single, many of whom chose that status.

The pervasive claims about the benefits of marrying are "social causation" explanations. There are variations in the ways that researchers describe social causation. Lamb, Lee, and DeMars (2003), for example, explain social causation this way: "...married persons

42

benefit directly from their relationships with their spouses, in terms of support, intimacy, caring, companionship, and the financial advantages that come with pooling resources...Marriage also has a buffering effect...by moderating the effects of events or circumstances that would result in lower well-being for unmarried persons" (p. 953).

Other scholars include "social control" among the causal mechanisms that account for why people who marry supposedly become healthier. For example, in a section called "The Virtues of Nagging," Waite and Gallagher (2000) declare: "Wives monitor both their own and their spouse's health habits. Wives not only discourage drinking, smoking, and speeding, but they cook low-fat or low-cholesterol meals, add more fruit and vegetables to the family diet, and encourage regular sleeping habits" (p. 55).

Most social causation explanations point to the resources that married people supposedly have that non-married people do not have. Sometimes a "crisis" perspective is added to the "resource" perspective to explain why divorced people sometimes fare less well than the currently married: "...married persons are healthier than persons who have transitioned out of marriage, because the stress of marital dissolution harms one's health..." (Carr & Springer, 2010).

There are at least four problems with social selection and social causation as the explanations for marital status differences. First, they cannot account for many of the actual research results. Second, they exclude other explanations. Third, the validity of marriage as the key construct has not been adequately established. Fourth, with its lopsided focus on the marital experience and neglect of the experience of single life, the framework is underdeveloped theoretically.

Results that Cannot Be Explained by the Purported Benefits of Marriage

The various components of the social causation hypothesis predict much more consistently positive, powerful, and unqualified effects than we find when we look closely at the available research results. They surely do not predict the results of the studies in which the always-single people fare better than the currently married. For example, if married people are so advantaged by the health-monitoring supposedly provided by their spouse, and all the fruits and vegetables purportedly getting included in all those healthful meals, then why are married people fatter than single people (Brown, Hockey, & Dobson,

2010; CDC, 2004)? Why do single people sometimes report better overall health than married people do (e.g., White, 1992)?

Consider, too, the results of a study of members of the military who were wounded after September 11, 2001 and asked about their physical and mental health in 2011 (Krull & Haugseth, 2012). Four groups were compared: married, divorced, separated, and always-single. The results were straightforward. The wounded warriors who had always been single fared best across a wide range of measures. They were least likely to report emotional or physical health problems that interfered with their work or other regular activities; least likely to have symptoms suggestive of PTSD; least likely to be depressed; least likely to be obese; and best able to bounce back from illness, injury, or hardship. If marriage provides more "support, intimacy, caring, [and] companionship" than single life, along with more buffering from the effects of hardship, and more beneficial social monitoring and control, then how is it possible that the single warriors did better than the married ones in so many ways?

The more sophisticated discussions of social causality allow for marital processes that are not uniformly positive. For example, in their discussion of social control, Carr and Springer (2010) note that "marriage may not necessarily promote good (or squelch bad) health behaviors, because spouses tend to share health behaviors..." (p. 750). Their discussion of psychosocial factors includes the possibility of social strain from conflict and negative behaviors as well as social support. The focus, though, is still on the experiences of married people and not single people.

Beyond Social Selection and Social Causation: Other Explanations

The social selection and social causation explanations of any marital advantages often omit other possibilities that have nothing to do with who gets married or stays married or what happens within a marriage. One of the most important of those alternative explanations is singlism – the stereotyping, stigmatizing, and discrimination against people who are single (DePaulo, 2006, 2011b; DePaulo & Morris, 2005). Perceptions of single people are harsher than those of married or coupled people, even in studies in which single and married people are described identically except for their marital status (e.g., DePaulo & Morris, 2006; Greitemeyer, 2009). In a random sample survey of

American adults, those who had always been single were much more likely that married people to report discriminatory treatment in informal interpersonal exchanges (Byrne & Carr, 2005). Single people are also targets of discrimination in the housing market (Morris, Sinclair, & DePaulo, 2007).

Some accounts of the resources available to married people, mentioned in social causation explanations, note that married people tend to be better off economically, and "to be insured, to have private health insurance, and to retain coverage upon job loss, drawing on their spouse's benefits..." (Carr & Springer, 2010). Those are important points. Left unstated, though, is the role of legal discrimination in producing these marital advantages. For example, lifelong single people with no children cannot leave their Social Security benefits to anyone else (they go back into the system), and no one else can will their Social Security benefits to lifelong single people. That's just one of the more than 1,000 federal statutes that benefit and protect only those who are legally married (Polikoff, 2008). In fact, the quest for access to these advantages has been one of the motivators of movement to legalize same-sex marriage. Many of these benefits are financial (such as a variety of tax breaks), and can amount to many thousands of dollars over a lifetime (Addo & Lichter, 2013). (Because the transition to getting married can result in significant financial advantages, it is not sufficient, in longitudinal studies, for researchers to control for economic variables only at the first wave of data collection.)

The important people in the lives of single people are left unrecognized and unprotected in other ways, too. For example, under the Family and Medical Leave Act (Family and Medical Leave Act, 1993), eligible employees are entitled to 12 weeks of unpaid leave "to care for the employee's spouse, child, or parent who has a serious health condition" or to deal with "a serious health condition that makes the employee unable to perform the essential functions of his or her job." The married person's spouse is covered under the Act. There is no equivalent person covered for single people. That means that single people cannot take time off under the Act to care for an important person in their life, such as a sibling or close friend; nor can such a person take time to care for them.

The flip side of singlism is important, too. Matrimania is the extreme valuing and celebration of marriage, couples, and weddings that is rampant in popular culture, the media, the workplace, the marketplace, politics, religion, and everyday life (DePaulo, 2006). Single people and single life are not accorded the same value or legitimacy. When people who marry get an initial boost in well-being that then dissipates, perhaps that honeymoon is attributable not (just) to the "support, intimacy, caring, [and] companionship" that they are supposedly getting because of being married, but to the fact that their life choice was just validated by other people, perhaps in a big, expensive celebration of themselves.

Singlism and matrimania pose significant questions for the study of the implications of marrying for health and well-being. For example, if single life were as valued and respected as married life, and if single people had access to the same benefits and protections as married people, how many people would choose to live single? How would the implications of marrying change?

If There Are Relationship Benefits, Can We Really Attribute Them Specifically to Marriage?

As cohabitation continues to grow in popularity, scholars sometimes ask whether the implications of marrying are unique to marriage, or whether they are similar for cohabitation. But adding cohabitation covers only a very limited range of the alternative ways in which the purported benefits of marriage might be obtained. Is it possible that people with one very close platonic friend, compared to people without any such friend, are happier, healthier, less depressed, have higher self-esteem, and live longer? Is it possible that those effects are stronger and less equivocal than the research evidence relevant to marrying? What about a more daring alternative – the possibility that what benefits people's health and well-being, and protects them against the slings and arrows of everyday life, is having not just one special person (whether a partner in marriage, cohabitation, or a close friend) but a network of diverse connections? Perhaps people are more resilient when they look to a number of different people, with different interests and resources, rather than just one significant other? There is, of course, a vast research literature on social support and social networks. What is missing is a sustained research inquiry that places social support networks alongside marriage and cohabitation and compares the implications for health and well-being.

Theoretical Neglect: The Study of Single Life

Single life is not just a place where people mark time until they marry. Many single people are living their lives fully and joyfully. Among relationship researchers and marriage scholars, single people should not just be conceptualized as the comparison group against which marriage is assessed. We need to think more deeply and theorize more seriously about the nature of single life, and especially about the aspects that have been so very neglected for so very long – the experiences of single life that make it so appealing. Once we realize what living single means to people who embrace their single lives, the questions we ask and the outcomes we measure will jump the typical boundaries of health and happiness.

From my pilot studies of people who are single at heart, and from more than a decade of writing for and about singles in the popular press as well as in academic journals, I want to suggest a beginning set of questions that scholars should consider posing in their studies of marital status and single life:

- How close are you to getting the amount of solitude that you desire?
- How close are you to getting the mix of time alone and time together that you consider ideal for you?
- How meaningful is your work? (A longitudinal study – Johnson, 2005 – suggests that single people value meaningful work more than married people do.)
- To what extent do you have a sense of self-determination? (Marks & Lambert, 1998, found that single people fared better than married people on autonomy.)
- To what extent do you have "a sense of continued growth and development as a person" (p. 657)? (Marks & Lambert, 1998, found that single people fared better than married people on personal growth.)
- To what extent are you pursuing your interests and your passions? To what extent are you doing so guiltlessly?
- To what extent can you save or spend your money as you see fit?
- To what extent have you been able to make the life choices that you find most fulfilling and most meaningful?

We also need to ask questions that recognize the ways in which single life is less valued and supported than married life. For example, we can ask single people whether they believe that their close friends are as valued as other people's romantic partners. Are they included in invitations to social events? Do other people ask about them? Do single people find that other important parts of their lives, such as their work, their interests, and their passions, are acknowledged by other people or are single people most often asked if they are seeing anyone?

We should also evaluate the range of competencies that single people have. Some marriage scholars have touted the efficiency that married couples enjoy by their division of labor; even among contemporary couples who embrace less gender-stereotyped divisions, one person might take care of some tasks, while the other specializes in different tasks. That may well have advantages while the union is intact, but what happens when it ends? Do single people – especially those who live alone – develop and maintain more different competencies in more different domains than married people do? Or are they more adept at finding help with the tasks they do not want to do on their own?

Perhaps because scholars have been so sure for so long that getting married makes people better off, they have focused on what they see as the strengths of married life and the risks of single life. We need to generate a more complete psychology. For example, our journals are stuffed with articles on loneliness but include far fewer offerings on the potential benefits of solitude and time alone. The literature on romantic relationship skills and successes is robust, but our understanding of the significance of adult friendship skills is far less developed. Yet, from the little research that is available, we already know that there are ways in which friendship skills are more important than romantic relationship skills (Roisman, Masten, Coatsworth, & Tellegen, 2004). Studies focusing on the relationship between two people in a couple, and no one else, are plentiful, but studies of the potential risks of intensive coupling are far less numerous. Yet there are indications that there could be important vulnerabilities. For example, in their study of different kinds of personal communities, Spencer and Pahl (2006) found that spouse/partner-based personal communities, in which "the partner is the focal point of the person's social world, acting as confidant, provider of emotional and practical support, and constant companion," were associated with lower scores on mental health measures.

Beyond the Question of Who Is Doing Better

One of the defining characteristics of contemporary life in Western societies is the explosion of choices about how to live. In the US, nuclear family households (married parents with dependent children) are outnumbered by households in which people live alone – and have been for years (DePaulo, 2006). Adults no longer need to get married or have children or live in the suburbs or follow any other pre-determined life path in order to live full, satisfying, and meaningful lives. They can choose the path that works for them.

As scholars, we should ask whether individual differences may be more important than we have acknowledged in conditioning the link between relationship or marital status and outcomes. As single life becomes a more viable option, individual preferences and characteristics may become more predictive of the implications of living single rather than getting married (or cohabiting). Already there is some suggestive evidence in support of that hypothesis of a fit between person and relationship/marital status. An example comes from a study of a nationally representative sample of Americans who were 40 and older and had been single their whole lives (Bookwala & Fekete, 2009) and a comparable sample of married people. The role of self-sufficiency differed for the two groups. For single people, the more self-sufficient they were, the less negative affect they experienced. For the currently-married people, the reverse was true: the more self-sufficient among them experienced more negative affect.

Such a research program on fit would acknowledge that people are not randomly assigned to marital status and they never will be. Although not everyone can have the marital status that they choose (some single people wish they were married, and some married people wish they were single even if they do not act on that wish), it is likely that choice has been playing an increasingly important role over time. As people become more free to pursue the way of living that best suits them, and scholars become more evenhanded in the attention they give to different life choices, our understanding of optimal experiences will deepen.

BELLA DePAULO

References

Addo, F. R. & Lichter, D. T. (2013). Marriage, marital history, and Black-White wealth differentials among older women. *Journal of Marriage and Family, 75*, 342-362.

Amato, P. R. (2010). Research on divorce: Continuing trends and new developments. *Journal of Marriage and Family, 72*, 650-666.

Anusic, I., Yap, S. C. Y., & Lucas, R. E. (2014a). Does personality moderate reaction and adaptation to major life events? Analysis of life satisfaction and affect in an Australian national sample. *Journal of Research in Personality, 51*, 69-77.

Anusic, I., Yap, S. C. Y., & Lucas, R. E. (2014a). Testing set-point theory in a Swiss national sample: Reaction and adaptation to major life events. *Social Indicators Research, 119*, 1265-1288.

Bookwala, J., & Fekete, E. (2009). The role of psychological resources in the affective well-being of never-married adults. *Journal of Social and Personal Relationships, 26*, 411-428.

Brockman, H., and Klein, T. (2004). Love and death in Germany: The marital biography and its effect on mortality. *Journal of Marriage and Family, 66*, 567-581.

Brown, S. L. (2003). Relationship quality dynamics of cohabiting unions. *Journal of Family Issues, 24*, 583-601.

Brown, W. J., Hockey, R., & Dobson, A. J. (2010). Effects of having a baby on weight gain. *American Journal of Preventative Medicine, 38*, 163-170.

Buettner, D. (2013, February/March). Give yourself a happiness makeover. *AARP: The Magazine*, 32-37.

Byrne, A., & Carr, D. (2005). Caught in the cultural lag: The stigma of singlehood. *Psychological Inquiry, 16*, 84-91.

Carr, D. & Springer, K. W. (2010). Advances in families and health research in the 21st century. *Journal of Marriage and Family, 72*, 743-761.

Census Bureau News (2014, July 30). Facts for features: Unmarried and Single Americans Week Sept. 21-27, 2014. Retrieved from http://www.census.gov/newsroom/facts-for-features/2014/cb14-ff21.html#.

Centers for Disease Control and Prevention. (2004). Marital status and health: United States, 1999-2002. Advance data, number 351. Hyattsville, MD:National Center for Health Statistics.

Day, M. V., Kay, A. C., Holmes, J. C., & Napier, J. L. (2011). System justification and the defense of committed relationship ideology. *Journal of Personality and Social Psychology*, 101, 291-306.

DePaulo, B. (2006). *Singled out: How singles are stereotyped, stigmatized, and ignored, and still live happily ever after.* New York: St. Martin's Press.

DePaulo, B. (2011a). Living single: Lightening up those dark, dopey myths. In W. R. Cupach and B. H. Spitzberg (Eds.), *The dark side of close relationships II* (pp. 409-439). New York: Routledge.

DePaulo, B. (2011b). *Singlism: What it is, why it matters, and how to stop it*. Charleston, SC: DoubleDoor Books.

DePaulo, B. (2012, May 10). What does it mean to be single at heart? *Psychology Today*. Retrieved from http://www.psychologytoday.com/blog/living-single/201205/what-does-it-mean-be-single-heart.

DePaulo, B. (2014). *The best of single life*. Charleston, SC: DoubleDoor Books.

DePaulo, B. M., & Morris, W. L. (2005). Singles in society and in science. *Psychological Inquiry*, *16*, 57-83.

DePaulo, B. M., & Morris, W. L. (2006). The unrecognized stereotyping and discrimination against singles. *Current Directions in Psychological Science*, *15*, 251-254.

Family and Medical Leave Act of 1993 (1993). The Family and Medical Leave Act of 1993. United States Department of Labor. Retrieved from http://www.dol.gov/whd/regs/statutes/fmla.htm.

Frech, A., & Williams, K. (2007). Depression and the psychological benefits of entering marriage. *Journal of Health and Social Behavior, 48*, 149-163.

Gerstel, N. (2011). Rethinking families and community: The color, class, and centrality of extended kin ties. *Sociological Forum*, *26*, 1-20.s

Gerstel, N., & Sarkisian, N. (2006). Marriage: The good, the bad, and the greedy. *Contexts*, *5*, 16-21.

Goldstein, J. R., & Kenney, C. T. (2001). Marriage delayed or marriage forgone? New cohort forecasts for first marriage of U. S. women. *American Sociological Review*, *66*, 506-519.

Gordon, S. (2008, August 11). Married folks still the healthiest. *Washington Post*. Retrieved from http://www.washingtonpost.com/wp-dyn/content/article/2008/08/11/AR2008081100632.html.

Gove, W. R., & Shin, H.-C. (1989). The psychological well-being of divorced and widowed men and women. *Journal of Family Issues*, *10*, 122-144.

Greitemeyer, T. (2009). Stereotypes of singles: Are singles what we think? *European Journal of Social Psychology*, *39*, 368-383.

Hawkley, L. C., Hughes, M. E., Waite, L. J., Masi, C. M., Thisted, R. A., & Cacioppo, J. T. (2008). From social structural factors to perceptions of relationship quality and loneliness: The Chicago Health, Aging, and Social Relations Study. *Journal of Gerontology: Social Sciences*, *63B*, S375-384.

Horwitz, A. V., White, H. R., & Howell-White, S. (1996). Becoming married and mental health: A longitudinal study of a cohort of young adults. *Journal of Marriage and the Family*, *58*, 895-907.

Johnson, M. K. (2005). Family roles and work values: Processes of selection and change. *Journal of Marriage and Family*, *67*, 352-369.

Johnson, N. J., Backlund, E., Sorlie, P. D., & Loveless, C. A. (2000). Marital status and mortality: The National Longitudinal Mortality Study. *Annals of Epidemiology*, *10*, 224-238.

Joung, I. M. A., van de Mheen, H. D., Stronks, K., van Poppel, F. W. A., & Mackenbach, J. P. (1998). A longitudinal study of health selection into marital transitions. *Social Science and Medicine*, *46*, 425-435.

Krull, H. & Haugseth, M. T. (2012). *Health and economic outcomes in the alumni of the Wounded Warrior Project*. Santa Monica, CA: RAND Corporation.

Lamb, K. A., Lee, G. R., & DeMaris, A. (2003). Union formation and depression: Selection and relationship effects. *Journal of Marriage and Family, 65*, 953-962.

Leddy, C. (2013, February 21). Money, marriage, kids. *Harvard Gazette*. Retrieved from http://news.harvard.edu/gazette/story/2013/02/money-marriage-kids/.

Liu, H., & Umberson, D. (2008). The times they are a changin': Marital status and health differentials from 1972 to 2003. *Journal of Health and Social Behavior, 49*, 239-253.

Lucas, R. E., Clark, A., Georgellis, Y., & Diener, E. (2003). Reexamining adaptation and the set point model of happiness: Reactions to changes in marital status. *Journal of Personality and Social Psychology, 84*, 527-539.

Luhmann, M., Hofmann, W., Eid, M., & Lucas, R. E. (2012). Subjective well-being and adaptation to life events: a meta-analysis. *Journal of Personality and Social Psychology, 102*, 592-615.

Marks, N. F., & Lambert, J. D. (1998). Marital status continuity and change among young and midlife adults: Longitudinal effects on psychological well-being. *Journal of Family Issues, 19*, 652-686.

Morris, W. L., Sinclair, S., & DePaulo, B. M. (2007). No shelter for singles: The perceived legitimacy of marital status discrimination. *Group Processes and Intergroup Relations, 10*, 457-470.

Musick, K., & Bumpass, L. (2012). Reexamining the case for marriage: Union formation and changes in well-being. *Journal of Marriage and Family, 74*, 1-18.

Parker-Pope, T. (2010). *For better: The science of a good marriage*. New York: Dutton Adult.

Perry v. Schwarzenegger (2010). 704 F. Supp. 2d 921 (Dist. Court, ND California 2010).

Polikoff, N. D. (2008). *Beyond (straight and gay) marriage: Valuing all families under the law*. Boston, MA: Beacon Press.

Rainie, L., & Malden, M. (2006). Romance in America. Pew Internet and American Life Program. www.PewInternet.org http://pewresearch.org/pubs/1/not-looking-for-love, Retrieved September 4, 2009.

Roisman, G. I., Masten, A. S., Coatsworth, J. D., & Tellegen, A. (2004). Salient and emerging developmental tasks in the transition to adulthood. *Child Development, 75*, 123-133.

Rook, K. S., & Zettel, L. A. (2005). The purported benefits of marriage viewed through the lens of physical health. *Psychological Inquiry, 16*, 116-121.

Spencer, L., & Pahl, R. (2006). *Rethinking friendship: Hidden solidarities today*. Princeton, NJ: Princeton University Press.

Taylor, P. (2010). *The decline of marriage and rise of new families*. Pew Research Center.

Umberson, D., Williams, K., Powers, D. A., Chen, M. D., & Campbell, A. M. (2005). As good as it gets? A life course perspective on marital quality. *Social Forces, 84*, 493-511.

Waite, L. J., & Gallagher, M. (2000). *The case for marriage: Why married people are happier, healthier, and better off financially*. New York: Doubleday.

Wang, W. & Parker, K. (2014, September). Record share of Americans have never married: as values, economics, and gender patterns change. Washington, D. C.: Pew Research Center's Social and Demographic Trends project.

White, J. M. (1992). Marital status and well-being in Canada. *Journal of Family Issues, 13*, 390-409.

Williams, K., & Umberson, D. (2004). Marital status, marital transitions, and health: A Gendered life course perspective. *Journal of Health and Social Behavior, 45*, 81-98.

Wu, Z., & Hart, R. (2002). The effects of marital and nonmarital union transition on health. *Journal of Marriage and Family, 64,* 420-432.

Yap, S. C. Y., Anusic, I., and Lucas, R. E. (2012). Does personality moderate reaction and adaptation to major life events? Evidence from the British Household Panel Survey. *Journal of Research in Personality, 46*, 477-488.

BELLA DePAULO

ABOUT THE AUTHOR

Bella DePaulo (Ph.D., Harvard University) writes myth-busting, consciousness-raising, totally unapologetic books on single life. The *Atlantic* magazine has described her as "America's foremost thinker and writer on the single experience."

Dr. DePaulo's books get much attention because of her expertise, her high profile in the media, and her years of writing for popular audiences. Her work has been described in the most influential newspapers, including *New York Times* (many times), the *Washington Post*, the *Wall Street Journal*, and *USA Today*, and in widely-read magazines such as the *New Yorker*, *Time*, *AARP Magazine*, *Newsweek / The Daily Beast*, the *Week*, the *Economist*, *More*, *Glamour*, *Cosmopolitan*, *Elle*, *Readers' Digest*, *Prevention*, the *Nation*, *Business Week*, *US News & World Report*, *Realtor Magazine*, the *Chronicle of Higher Education*, and the *Atlantic*. Many newspapers and magazines around the world have also discussed her ideas. Bella DePaulo has been writing the "Living Single" blog for *Psychology Today* since 2008. She also blogs for PsychCentral and has contributed to the Huffington Post. She has appeared many times on radio and television.

Bella DePaulo is the winner of the Excellence in Research Award, bestowed by the American Association for Single People. The author of more than 100 scholarly publications, including more than a dozen books, she has also won two prestigious academic awards, the Research Scientist Development Award and the James McKeen Cattell Award. Professor DePaulo has served in leadership positions in professional organizations and has served on the editorial boards of many journals. She is currently a Project Scientist in the psychology department at the University of California at Santa Barbara. Visit Dr. DePaulo's website at www.BellaDePaulo.com.